Thank You For Sharing, Lord

by

Doris M. Whitney

MOORLEY'S Print & Publishing

ISBN 0 86071 425 X

MOORLEY'S Print & Publishing

23 Park Rd., Ilkeston, Derbys DE7 5DA

Tel/Fax: (0115) 932 0643

NOTE FROM THE AUTHOR

I use this little book for epilogues, coffee mornings and similar gatherings. Something short but thoughtful proves acceptable. It could also be used for private devotions.

Working through the Old Testament characters we find they always needed God to sustain them. In the New Testament we see Jesus and his followers going through similar experiences. They too needed God all the time. Frank and open prayers bring us into the picture.

D.M.W.

Dedicated to my precious grandchildren:
Jonathan, Alexander, Anastasia, Josie, David, Eleanor
and Richard.

My love to all of you in Christ Jesus.

1 Cor. 16:24 (N.I.V.)

LOOK BACK - GO FORWARD

Genesis 13:3-4

Abraham is portrayed as a man who obeyed God's command to go forward. There was, however, one moment when even he had to go back. Soon after Abraham accepted his instructions to go out and face the unknown, he built an altar at a place called Ai. Then he had to flee from famine, face a period when his spiritual life was at a low ebb and know the special temptations that come from prosperity. At this point Abraham went back to Ai *"where his tent had been at the beginning"*. From there he gathered fresh strength from God to face the next stage of his journey.

John 10:22 and 40

We often think of Jesus within a setting of Palestinian sunshine. Yet we read of a day when Jesus stood in the Temple porch *"and it was winter"*. We feel it was also a winter of the spirit which Jesus was going through and this had proved distressing indeed. Jesus faced a hostile crowd and not one person would stand by him. Eventually the watching crowd withdrew and Jesus was able to escape. He went back to the river Jordan *"where he had been baptised"*. There Jesus was refreshed and able to take up his calling again.

Prayer

You have called me to go forward, Lord. I have not always obeyed so it is with some relief I admit I'm glad you sometimes suggest I go back. Even this isn't always easy. There have been days in my life which I couldn't possibly face living over again. Yet I long to live happy moments once more, though experience has taught me this may not be a success. Places change. So do people. Even more, so do I. I find it helpful to go back to times when you gave me what I needed rather than what I wanted. I confess I've often been afraid of what a day might hold for me. When you chose to take the object of fear away I have thought of Mary worrying over that big stone in front of your tomb. Often on days of unbearable loneliness you have filled the dreadful gap and I have been comforted. Take me on or back, Lord.....whatever is best. But please keep tight hold of me. AMEN.

JOYS OF INHERITANCE

Genesis 26:12-18

Abraham and Sarai both laughed when Isaac was promised to them. It had seemed so unlikely they would have a child. In fact, the promise being fulfilled was essential to the continuance of the line. The most important facts about Isaac were his birth and his marriage. He did, however, do other things which were blest. Water was very short in the desert through which he travelled and the enemy had stopped up all the wells. Isaac re-dug the wells of his father and this typified the way in which he showed he was thankful for his inheritance.

Matthew 5:1-9

Jesus talked a lot about people who had an inheritance. In Bible language this meant something promised beforehand by God. It was not the rich and the prosperous who would receive great rewards, but rather those who had accepted self-discipline. Nobody becomes meek, merciful or pure in heart unless they submit their lives to God's control. These are the people who will inherit the kingdom and they are often to be found in the most unlikely places.

Prayer

You have been very kind in giving me so many wonderful people to share my life, Lord. Christian parents cared for me and educated me at great cost to themselves. Wise teachers and church friends not only shared their knowledge of the scriptures but also brought me nearer to you by the way they lived. Remind me it is now my turn to help those who depend on me to know you and take your values into their lives. Let me not worry only about passing on material security but show me how to be a good influence in all that matters most. Remind me that the priority for you, Lord, was living close to your Father and helping others to do the same. Problems arise when I think of my weakness and forget your strength. I use up too much energy by worrying. Let that be a point where I meet up with someone I can help. I see my family as a very precious inheritance and my friends as wonderful "extras". May I treasure them. Most of all, let them know they are priceless to you. AMEN.

LET ME FIRST.....

Genesis 32:24-26

Jacob spent a lot of his life running away. He ran from his brother whom he had cheated and his brother-in-law after robbing him. He tried to run from his conscience and his God. However, God found a way to get through to this man whom scripture lines up with the patriarchs. Even in his dreams Jacob was reminded there are strong links between earth and heaven. One night Jacob fought for hours against an unknown assailant and that was the moment when he tried to bargain with God. He promised he would stop resisting if God blessed him first. Many times this man had to accept it is God who lays down conditions. Man's duty is to obey.

Luke 14:18-20

There were plenty of people willing to follow Jesus on their own terms. The rich young ruler would have gone willingly had he been certain of keeping his bank balance intact. There were others who quickly thought of excuses to give themselves time to think a bit longer. So often people have almost followed our Lord, but felt they must safeguard other matters first. Jesus was not being heartless when he asked for unconditional surrender. This was what he was going to give out of love for us all.

Prayer

I've sometimes been foolish enough to try to escape you, Lord. This may be because of a guilty conscience because I knew I had failed you. Quite often I've turned my back on you because I knew you were looking for something to be done or said. I pretended I hadn't noticed. I've often sung that hymn about giving myself to you "in full and glad surrender". I've known I should stop singing because my surrender wasn't complete and I certainly wasn't glad about it. The moment I think of your cross, Lord, my whole attitude changes. You gave everything in love to those who had betrayed you and that includes me. Deep down I know I could never repay you but I feel so mean when I give you very meagre offerings. I don't really want to run away from you, Lord. When I do, I want to go home again before bed-time. I am trying to surrender to your will. This means asking you yet again to take over mine. I may have to ask you to break me..... until it hurts. Then I know you will stay near to heal and forgive. AMEN.

GOD'S CHOICE

Genesis 48:8-14

Stories of Joseph were very familiar to us when we were small. The spoilt boy grew to responsible manhood and had many important tasks to do for his nation and his God. There was one day when God took the efficient Joseph by surprise. Joseph had taken his two sons to old father Jacob expecting the old man to place his hands in blessing on the older boy, thereby denoting he was to be the important one. But Jacob crossed his hands over and blessed Ephraim, the younger son. Several times in the Bible we read how men decided God would act, but they were reminded God often had ideas of his own.

Luke 6:12-16

Jesus prayed all through the night before he chose his disciples. Yet we are amazed at some of the people who are found on the list. It is doubtful whether we would have chosen any one of them to help with the mammoth task of establishing God's kingdom on earth. We realise, however, these men were God's choice and it is in his nature to choose ordinary folk to do extraordinary things. So often Jesus presented a big challenge to most unlikely people. It is good they became new people as they offered their lives in love and service.

Prayer

I like to be on the front row when you are giving out blessings, Lord. What is more, I like to choose the blessing, forgetting I may be depriving someone else. My longing for blessings often includes special privileges. I fancy certain tasks I could do for you and have been known to ride rough-shod over someone far more suitable. I've been thinking a lot about those disciples you chose to help when you started to preach about the kingdom. They were a very strange bunch - not one of them all that reliable when it came to the test. I'm so glad they came back once they realised you had overcome death and you helped them to become such wonderful leaders of your church. That gives me hope, Lord.....hope that in spite of all my failings you still want me to work for you. It also gives me certainty as once I have truly accepted your leadership you will lead me forward and place me in the task you have marked out for me. Help me to be unselfish in my service to you. Keep me alert and waiting, Lord. Be patient with me as I try to learn when I should step back or go on. AMEN.

WHY ME?

Exodus 3:11-12

Moses was a born leader but there was a day when he felt he could not do what God asked from him. *"Go speak to the Pharaoh,"* said God, and Moses replied he was unable to talk. We feel he was trying to persuade himself the job was not for him. Yet many times later we find Moses had a great deal to say. We are glad he was not dismissed from service at his time of weakness and to this day we are able to find a great deal of help in the words of Moses. We have to admit much of his teaching is rather negative. We are glad to turn to the more positive commands Jesus gave.

John 5:2-9

Jesus did more than anybody else to help the weak. Those who hesitated to follow were challenged. Those who felt they could not even stand up were told to stand and walk. Jesus helped them, but also made plain people were to try and use their own strength. The man who hid his solitary talent was told he should have used it and looked for results. Jesus said even people who had limited sight and hearing would find those gifts enhanced if they used them. Our Lord dealt firmly with weakness of character and even the most unpromising of his followers eventually grew strong enough to face the big tests and win.

Prayer *I find it so comforting you did not take the easy way, Lord. You could have escaped your difficulties. Forgive me if I say I'm glad you almost said "No" to the bitter cup of suffering, but your determination to do the Father's will soon took over again. Thankyou too that in your victory you also made mine possible. I want to say sorry for all those times when I have turned away from you. At those points I was thinking more about my weakness than your strength. Next time I am tempted I want you to come with me right up against the problem. It would be so easy to run and to go on running, but I want to remember that whatever is hurting me has hurt you far more and you faced up to it all. You did not promise an easy time when we try to witness for you. That's fair enough when you had everything so hard. Help me to steer clear of obvious temptations. Looking at whatever is tempting me is quite enough to make me fail. I want to look to you and keep on looking until things are easier. I know every victory opens up the way for another one and I praise you for that. AMEN.*

TAKING RESPONSIBILITY

Exodus 19:1-6

God had a lot to teach his people about how he would take care of them. He went ahead to show the way, provided competent leaders, but also made plain he did not intend to carry them without any effort on their part. God reminded the people of Israel how the eagle carried her young. When the baby bird seemed ready to take to the air the mother bird would fly underneath. She was still near enough to help if the baby lost his nerve. Thus God would take care of his people. They must do much for themselves but he was never too far away in case things went wrong.

Matthew 25:14-27

Jesus called men to serve him and then trained them to become fully equipped. For encouragement he told the story of the talents. The master did not stand over those he trusted but expected much from them. On another occasion Jesus talked of a man who put his servants in charge of his vineyard and then left them to it. Even Jesus was answerable to God and only with his last breath did he feel the task was finished. We cannot even begin ours without asking for his help.....but begin we must or we shall disappoint him.

Prayer

Thank you, Lord, that you have always encouraged your followers to take responsibility. I can think of many who turned their back on safety and went into difficult circumstances in your name. I look with wonder at the leaders of the Early Church and realise how dependent they were on your Spirit to help and inspire them. Yet even though you often opened up the way, you still expected people to show some initiative and to make some decisions. May I realise I must not sit down and wait for your kingdom to come in our midst. You want action as well as prayer. You need me to speak as well as listen. I am very grateful you do not treat me like a puppet even though I know you will be near in every choice I make. Let me look at your service to God over and over again, Lord. You tried so hard to help people take responsibility but they were a very long time before they would. As you left them you must have known you were taking a risk in depending on them to continue your work. I am often as frail as that, Lord. Please strengthen me so I can look you in the face and receive your "Well Done". AMEN.

GLIMPSE OF GOD

Exodus 19:16-21

Moses was allowed to speak to God but not see him. So many times in the wilderness story the people saw evidence of what God was doing but were told not to attempt to go anywhere near him. This was quite in keeping with the beliefs of the time and many years were to pass before anyone realised God was approachable and would even give a welcome. However, all through those years there was nothing lacking on God's part. He was always concerned and loving. Over and over again he forgave those who strayed away. God has been the same from the beginning. It is our attitude towards him that must change and develop.

John 14:8-11

It was Jesus who helped men see God. His disciples continually questioned as to what God was like. Jesus said quite simply, *"See me and you see the Father"*. If we think quietly through the life of our Lord and see this as a gradual revelation of God, we shall find there is nothing more we need know. This does not mean God will not use other ways to help our understanding. The disciples often helped each other. Even now, every kindly act tells us a little more about a loving God. But the supreme example is always Jesus. Look away from him and we turn our backs to God.

Prayer

I am looking at you, Lord, and feeling so grateful this helps me know God better. I see you dealing with people in pain and realise how much God cares. I hear you teaching me and so opening up new thoughts about God's purpose for all our lives. I remember you gave yourself for our sins and I try to take in how far God is willing to go out of love for his children. I am holding on to your promise to be with us for always and am so glad this means I can live with God believing he will never let go. Yet I know this is a challenge to the way I live as well as a comfort. I cannot do anything mean or selfish without realising you are nearby and what I do will hurt you as well as somebody else. When I am attacked by temptation I know I can stretch out a hand and touch you and this goes a long way towards helping me overcome. I want you to help me as I try to grow in wisdom and faith. I want to be aware of you more and more clearly. May I be genuine in my thanks for this great privilege. AMEN.

CONSTANT PRESENCE

Exodus 33:7-10

The Israelites were often rebellious when they travelled across the wilderness to their promised land. However, God stayed with them and in their better moments they realised the importance of his being there. After the first Covenant they wanted to cherish their laws, though they were not always keen to obey them. They built a portable tabernacle with its ark to carry the law and felt that as long as this stayed with them they could step out into the future, confident God was at their side.

John 20:26-28

Thomas was one of the Lord's disciples who badly needed Jesus' physical presence to sustain his faith. He and his friends had to learn that after the resurrection Jesus was still with them but in a different kind of way. He was no longer limited by bodily constrictions so he could be by their side anywhere and everywhere and at any time. Only thus was Jesus free to keep his wonderful promise to be with those who loved him to the end of time. Jesus made plain this does not apply only to our present life. Beyond that there is eternity with his Father.

Prayer

I love the stories about your hands, Lord. I remember you touched blind eyes and made them see. You lifted up a little girl and an old lady giving them new strength to live. You broke bread in the Emmaus travellers' home just as you did in the Upper Room with your disciples. It must have meant so much to be touched by you, knowing this meant you were very, very near. I find myself thinking on to that dreadful moment when wicked men drove nails into your hands in spite of all the love they had given to needy people. Yet in the end the triumph was yours. Even though you passed through all the glory of the resurrection you prepared a fish breakfast for tired and hungry men and allowed Thomas to touch you with his hands. Yet you had a challenging word to say to Thomas. You said your followers could go on to believe in you even though they would not be able to see and touch you. That must have been hard at first but I'm glad they managed it because I must learn the same lesson. Thank you, Lord that I can feel you near and rich joy can be mine forever. AMEN.

BE OF GOOD COURAGE

Joshua 7:6-10

Joshua was told by God to be brave. He was also commissioned to remind the people they too could be strong if they remembered God was always with them, yet we have one picture of Joshua prostrate with grief and even tearing his clothes in anguish. At times he even wished he could go back to slavery. He was very depressed when he was told to sort out which family was bringing disgrace on the company. At this point God reminded Joshua he had never been promised the way would be easy. We know the hardest tasks often come when we are travelling through a wilderness of some kind or another.

Matthew 5:10-11

The followers of Jesus had to be reminded his teaching was aimed at telling them how to face day to day problems as well as a frightening future. Like us, they had to learn the teachings of Jesus are not always pleasant. Jesus saw tribulation ahead for himself and those who tried to walk in his footsteps. Testing times always seemed to be just around the corner for our Lord and his companions. They had to learn difficulties which were just as much a part of the Christian way as were blessings. The fact that Jesus has been through them makes all the difference.

Prayer *I am trying to praise you, Lord, that being loyal in your service may sometimes mean the going is tough. Thank you that whatever I have to go through, you have been there before and you conquered, however difficult the trial. Thank you too for those days when I feel I could tackle anything in your name. I will try to see some sense in discipline and disappointment. I need you to keep telling me you promised to share the whole of life with me. I want you to make me aware you are still near when the future seems clouded in mists of uncertainty. I know you will make the next step plain and we can then go on together from there. Sometimes when I listen to the news reports it appears there is so much wrong with our world. You made it and said it was good. I hope you can still think the same about us and that is the side I want you to help me with. Show me how to look away when temptations come. Help me to go on trusting even when the day seems to be going wrong. Help me take every opportunity to do good deeds, even little ones, and may the result be someone is a little nearer your kingdom. AMEN.*

PEACEMAKER

Judges 4:4-9

Deborah lived a useful life. She was nurse as well as judge and prophetess. When on duty Deborah sat under a palm tree and was consulted by various Israelite tribes when they had disputes. This woman was very brave too. When an army chief consulted her about going into battle, she offered to go into the thick of the fray with him. Deborah was eventually buried under another tree near Bethel. As she is mentioned as Rebekah's nurse, it seems likely she was present at the eventful birth of Jacob and Esau.

John 20:19-22

The word *"peace"* occurs in every book of the New Testament. We associate it with the teaching of Jesus and think of it as part of the legacy he left to those he loved. Later Paul greeted the Churches with peace and left it with them as a benediction. Neither Jesus nor Paul would have thought of peace as merely an absence of strife. Christian peace is something positive and constructive. This often means action on our part and Jesus made plain he left his blessing on all who tried.

Prayer

I want to thank you, Lord, for all those days when I feel I am living in your peace. I feel calm and contented and it is easy then to be nice to other people. But I know you are not deceived into thinking I am always like that. I'm only too aware of many a battle that started inside me and anyone I met up with was likely to get the over-flow. It serves me right if I don't know peace again until I've said "I'm sorry" to you and the person I've hurt. I want you to fill my mind with thoughts about positive acts of peace. Show me where to go and then please open up opportunities for me to calm someone down and help them start again. Yet I must be kind about that, Lord. It's not for me to go around looking for people I judge to be in the wrong. I'm only too aware I need your discipline every day and all day so I can do something good and speak kindly. I am amazed you were always so gentle and yet so strong. Many people would not let you lead them into peaceful thinking. I too often find it easier to raise my voice and then try to say something clever which I know perfectly well will cause pain. Be very near in all my words and actions please, Lord. Only then can I think of myself as a child of God. AMEN.

YOUR GOD.....MY GOD

Ruth 4:13-22

Most people know how thoughtful Ruth was towards her mother-in-law. We know too about Naomi's courage in going back to Bethlehem when her life had changed so much she felt her very name should be altered. We may need a reminder that the most important fact of this story emerges at the end. Ruth eventually married her kinsman, Boaz, and their little son was to play an important part in God's plan for the nation. We need to note that what we call a mixed marriage took place when there was an almost fanatical attempt to keep the Jewish strain pure. God had set his sights much further than that.

John 4:1-10

We feel Jesus knew he should go through Samaria, probably sensing he would meet someone who badly needed a contact. There were other occasions when our Lord made plain he did not adopt the usual attitude of Jews towards Samaritans. Jesus knew exactly what the woman at the well was like in character as well as in her secret life. Yet he used her to do some missionary work. It is for God to decide who will be given a particular responsibility and he often surprises us by his choice. The vision of all nations before God's throne in heaven was in God's mind long before man thought of it.

Prayer

I have often thought, Lord, what an important baby you were. It was a strange way for God to let his people know he loved them, but it worked. I turn my mind back into history and think of that other baby born to Ruth and Boaz. He was destined to begin the line of David which eventually led to your coming on earth. The idea that you plan events such a long time beforehand helps me realise what an Almighty One you are. Yet, thinking of all those babies, and all that could have gone wrong, I realise how tender is your care over us. Each day somebody had to respond to their needs and, as they grew to manhood, the responsibility would increase. I find myself asking whether you have plans for our lives a long time ahead. I can look back and see something of how things have worked out for me and I'm only a very ordinary person. Best of all, I'm so grateful it was out of love for your world that all this happened. Your world means people and I'm so grateful to be one of them. I want you to look after me today please, not just because I need you now but because I realise the simple happenings of today might have a telling influence on what is to come. AMEN.

SYMPATHETIC COMFORT

1 Samuel 1:12-17

Hannah was so sad her prayers would not go into words. It was only because the old priest was very sympathetic that he was able to share her sorrow. It was a good thing Hannah made the effort to go to the Temple, although this was obviously one of the places where she suffered most. Hannah was only allowed one piece of meat at the time of the offering because she was only one and had no offspring. However, God had his plans ready to answer this woman's prayers. Hannah did have a son and, when he was still quite small, he was soon enrolled to play a very responsible part in God's ideas for the nation.

Luke 7:11-15

The widow of Nain is one of the most pathetic people in the gospel story. Jesus arrived at her village in time to see the widow's eldest son being carried off to his burial. The household was so poor she could not even afford a coffin. Jesus gave comfort first and then restored the boy back to life. Our Lord showed tremendous insight for the situation. This is not surprising as he came to this world to share every aspect of human life. Before long he was able to go through death himself outside a city wall. Maybe he was a little more prepared as he watched the widow's son being carried through the gates at Nain.

Prayer

I'm thankful we do not have to tell you about our deepest sorrows, Lord. Through sharing our life, you know all about the hurts which cannot be expressed and the pains from which we can rarely find relief. I want you to use all my sad times to help me be more understanding with others. May I find ways in which even my saddest days can be lived to your glory. This is hard because it means putting myself to the back of the picture - but you know all about that. There are times when I seem to be in the dark for hours on end. I need you so much to help me open my eyes and focus them on somebody else's pain. I know, in my better moments, your love for me can send light into the darkest tunnel. From that point I want you to help me look to the future. Help me to be sure there are still things I can do for you and other people, even when my strength seems much too limited. Many of my sorrows spring from the fact that I love someone a lot. Yet love is a wonderfully positive thing and I want you to keep reminding me of that. Today's dark patch could pave the way for extra light tomorrow..... that is, if I can hand it over to you. AMEN.

ALERT TO GOD

1 Samuel 3:1-8

Samuel was trained to listen to the voices of God almost from babyhood. God seems to have used the opportunity to give Samuel a difficult task to do. His first commission was to tell the old priest bad news about his sons. Later on, Samuel's own sons disappointed him. Several times the grown up Samuel had to bear the brunt of mistakes made by the people and their king. However carefully Samuel listened to God as he prayed, this did not mean the answer was always easy. When God is trying to lead a nation to know him better, there are often individuals who suffer in the process.

Matthew 3:13-17

Several times we read in the gospels that God spoke directly to Jesus. This must have been a tremendous source of strength to him. Jesus had taken on everything involved in living our life and we all know this meant suffering, pain and sorrow. Had Jesus not shared fully in all this he would not have been the wonderful help he is. Close though Jesus was to his Father, this did not mean his problems faded away. In the midst of it all Jesus trained himself to understand what God was saying and doing through all the hurt. We are a long way from trusting our Lord like that but he will help us if we try.

Prayer

I'm very good at listening to voices, Lord. The trouble is, they contradict each other. My friends mean well but often they pull me in too many directions. When I have a problem, I know in my heart there is only one way through. This may be obvious if I have known the experience before, but as I try to mature in my Christian faith, difficulties come which I did not even realise existed. You talked about being the Way and Truth, Lord. Maybe the reason I get myself into so many muddles is because I listen to too many voices instead of concentrating on what you are trying to tell me. Where did you go for help, Lord? I believe it was to your Father. When you talked about being my Way I am trying to see you meant the Way to God. I know the answer to everything that perplexes me is there with him, so I want you to help me get there, and stay with me, so we can see the way forward together. Thankyou for being the Truth, too, Lord. So many clamouring voices claim to have true knowledge about how we should live, but their sound is just noise. I need to turn away from them towards your gentle but firm leading which has helped me so many times before. AMEN.

STAY MY HAND

1 Samuel 14:36-37

King Saul had to face many battles during his rather tempestuous reign. At one point he wanted to attack the Philistines during the night but the priest advised him to pray first. God did not give Saul the answer he wanted that day and this was not the only time he had to be restrained from hasty action. So very often Saul disappointed God and there are moments in his story when we almost feel God must have regretted giving him responsibility. Saul let down Samuel, David and many others, but worst of all, he betrayed the trust placed in him by God.

Luke 9:51-56

We usually think of James and John as amongst the more obedient of our Lord's followers. Yet one day Jesus called them *"sons of thunder."* Jesus often needed people to respond to a need by a quick action, but on this occasion he had to hold them back. Jesus said a very firm *"No"* when these two men wanted to call down fire on a Samaritan village. Jesus tried to teach them that Samaritans, like everybody else, needed to be loved, not forced, into the kingdom he came to establish. A kingdom that lived by force would not have Jesus to rule over it. He could be very strong when the occasion demanded it, but everything he did was regulated by his love for his Father and his people.

Prayer

I've prayed for courage many a time, Lord, but I know sometimes I must ask that you will hold me back. Forgive me when I am headstrong and disobedient and help me to develop a quiet trust in your guidance so I can be sure it is your will I'm carrying out and not my own. Be very near to me when I have a difficult decision, to make sure I have time to ask myself whether my action might hurt someone very badly. You touched so many people's lives but not once did you leave someone wishing they had not met you because you were unkind. I need to learn to live at your pace and develop wise discernment in every testing situation. Forgive me for being wilful and headstrong when it would be much better to go steady. Remind me not to be so anxious to carry out my own plans that I quite forget you may wish to take me in a totally different direction. If I have hurt someone, Lord, please take me that way again. Then I can say sorry and do something kind and thoughtful. Maybe I can swallow my pride and let them do something for me. AMEN.

GOD'S PRIORITIES

2 Samuel 7:1-7

King David's conscience gave him trouble when he realised he was living in rather a splendid palace. He thought of his God living in the temporary dwelling of a tent. David consulted the prophet Nathan, and between them they decided it would be a good thing for the king to build a Temple. But overnight the situation changed. Nathan received a vision from God and it became clear David was not the one chosen to build the House of the Lord. God's priorities for David at that point were much more in the realm of character building.

Acts 16:7-10

Paul's diary must have been very full. His missionary journeys were carefully planned so that strategic places in the known world would hear the gospel. At one point God gave Paul a vision through which it was made plain there must be a change of direction. Paul was called over to Europe where the gospel was eventually to make many conquests. Every missionary journey, in fact every task we do for God, is very important. He always helps his servants to decide what the next move should be.

Prayer

I've made a big mistake today, Lord. I expressed an opinion without really thinking what I was saying. I was anxious not to appear ignorant but now I feel rather foolish. This has reminded me of all the times I have acted without praying enough first. My decisions are too often coloured by my desires and so I speak and act when it would have been far better to wait a bit. I know you want me to tell others about my faith in you, but I can so easily do more harm than good if I forget to wait for your guidance before I speak or move. It could be you have something more urgent lined up for me. It could be you have someone else in mind for the job that attracts me. I realise it is so necessary to place myself entirely in your hands. My task is to be ready when you speak and then make sure what I do next is your will and not always mine. The disciples came to you over and over again to receive your orders for the day. Sometimes they tried to go ahead of you and more than once they did something which could easily have hindered the progress of your kingdom. They were wisest when they stayed near you, Lord, and I know that is true for me too. AMEN.

WISDOM FOR UNDERSTANDING

1 Kings 3:5-12

Solomon's prayer was for wisdom. This rather suggests a humble attitude which was not always very obvious in his character. A reading of this king's story reveals he took good care to add to his own prestige with every move he made. At times he did appear to be wise but then was foolish enough to worship at heathen shrines while at the same time professing allegiance to God. Being born into a rich household meant Solomon was never very close to his people, many of whom were still shepherds.

Mark 10:13-16

The followers of Jesus were called disciples, so it is not surprising they always had a lot to learn. Sometimes their methods were wrong; very often their actions were not in line with what our Lord wanted to do for those who needed him. At one point, when Jesus wanted people to realise how much they didn't know, he pointed to the children. They would never have claimed to have the answers to all life's problems. They would question, wonder and trust. Every sincere follower of Jesus needs to do just that all through their lives.

Prayer

It's a good thing you can over-rule my mistakes, Lord. However many times I let you down, your love for me helps me try again. I am so thankful you hold the world in your hands. Our world must often grieve you and I contribute quite a lot to your hurt and disappointment. Because of your care for me I know something positive can come out of my mistakes. I want you to help me always to be willing to learn from what I do wrong. So often I fail because I don't have enough patience. So often I try to be too clever. I need you to steady me, make me think out what I intend to do and not even attempt it until I feel you approve. I can look back to many times when I have rushed into some piece of service. I realise now I needed to wait until I was quite sure this was what you wanted from me. Your disciples had to learn this. Like me, they wanted quick results but you talked to them quietly about seeds growing in secret and silent leaven working through the dough. I need that teaching and more, Lord. I need to grow wiser and understand your methods rather than push my own. AMEN.

WAY OF COMPROMISE

1 Kings 15:16-19

King Asa started his reign well by removing heathen shrines. He was particularly ruthless with private shrines belonging to his mother in law. Then the weaker side of his character became apparent when he had a threat of war and tried to bribe Syria to help him. The bribe he chose was to offer gold and silver vessels from the House of the Lord. This was inexcusable as God had already given Asa a victory over a much more powerful enemy. Serving God one minute and working against him the next can only lead to disaster.

Matthew 5:27-30

Nobody knew better than Jesus that it is fatal to compromise with evil. He said it is not wise even to take a look at things which may prove to be a snare. Each of us must decide this particular point for ourselves and this may often call for severe personal discipline. Jesus makes very plain that anything which could develop into a stumbling block in the way of our following God's plan must be cut out while there is still time. A mere glance or two in the wrong direction can be the beginning of some compromise or even failure.

Prayer

I want to ask you to take charge of my thoughts, Lord - even my most secret thoughts. I am so thankful I can ask you to help with the little niggling temptations which come every day as well as turning me right round when I have to fight something really hard. I realise many of my battles are about things and people I care about very much. I feel it was like that with you. You wanted to feed the people so changing those stones to bread would seem an easy way. You wanted the world for your kingdom and I feel it must have been so difficult to turn your back on a spectacular way to get it. One of my problems is that I decide whatever tempts me won't make much difference to the world as a whole. Then I realise if everybody thought like that, we should all be on a downward slope. Help me to bring you in right at the beginning of my temptations, Lord, or rather, remind me that you are there already. If I act as I shouldn't, you are the first person to be hurt. Please fill my mind with lovely thoughts and make it a suitable dwelling for you.....then please live there, Lord, and so stay very near. AMEN.

TO WITNESS IS TO SUFFER

1 Kings 19:12-15

Elijah was a man of outstanding courage. He dared to challenge a wicked king and queen to mend their ways. He also had a very strong constitution and tremendous energy. He could win a race against chariot horses and yet fast for long periods. There was one point where Elijah's faith in God wavered. He suffered from acute depression and became very lonely. He went away to the Holy Mountain and there God gave him encouragement to go back and witness to the people equipped with newly-found strength.

Acts 7:54-60

Stephen was a faithful follower of our Lord and quite expected to go through a time of suffering. Chosen to do social work in the Early Church, Stephen's name soon became known. It was, however, as a preacher that he upset a whole lot of people, and in the end, some of them stoned him to death. Yet, because this remarkable man spoke out so bravely, there were wonderful consequences to his actions. His witness proved very painful but because of it the beginnings of the Christian mission were only just around the corner.

Prayer

I find it very easy to come to you for strength and comfort, Lord, but I sometimes put off my prayers if I know you are going to ask something difficult. I claim to be a Christian soldier but complain when I receive the first tiny wound. Remind me you never said following you would be easy. Those tests seem to keep coming. Sometimes I am ready, but more often I am caught unawares. I realise now why you told your followers they must watch and pray all the time. I quickly get into difficulties if there is some unexpected evil in a situation I thought was safe. At that point I often realise you had given me a lot of warnings. Forgive me for failing because I know what you want me to do will cost me a lot and may even hurt. At those points I need you to take me back to Calvary. You knew it would hurt and the cost would be your life. Thinking like that makes me feel ashamed, I give in so easily. Your love for us all was so strong you opened your arms to accept the suffering. I want you to help me do the same without grumbling and complaining. The worst I can endure is so little compared with what you did for me. AMEN.

TASK COMPLETED

2 Kings 4:42-44

Neither Elijah nor Elisha were able to complete the task given them to do. Even after they both died there were still many heathen shrines left in Israel. They did, however, make some progress in their efforts to help the people see they should be worshipping the One True God. Many other prophets were to be called to the same type of witness and occasionally we get a little glimpse into the future. Elisha fed one hundred men with twenty barley loaves. Much later on, Jesus was to feed thousands with only five. Great wonders were on the way and many of these had small beginnings.

John 19:25-30

Jesus had many set-backs but at the end of his life he was able to say *"It is finished"*. This did not mean there was nothing left to do towards the establishment of God's kingdom on earth. Jesus meant his task of ensuring man's salvation was complete. There was just nothing left to offer in the way of remedial love. Then it became necessary for mankind to accept this wonderful offering. Each must take and thankfully receive for himself. Jesus completed his part, but there are many, many people who have never said *"Thank you"*.

Prayer

I am sometimes amazed, Lord, that you left work like your own for us to do. I realise my part may be very small, but it still matters. One lovely thing about it is that my fellow Christians and I can join together in serving you. Even you needed friends around you and this is more needful for us. Help me to see where my service can fit in with others. Let me not get in their way or try to override them for my own glory. Show us how we can get together and, over and over again, we would ask you to direct and guide us, so we may not hinder your master plan for our world. I want to say I am sorry for all those times when I know I have been a hindrance. Sometimes I get side-tracked and busy myself with something which will do no good for anybody. On my lazy days I stop and start, or sometimes just stop. Remind me Lord how you went to the help of poorly folk even at the end of a long day's work. You made time to pray very early in the morning. Please give me, and those who share my service, persistence to keep on.....and even then to try again. AMEN.

THE GIFT OF HEALING

2 Kings 5:1-14

The story of Naaman the leper is one of the few about healing in the Old Testament. Had this man lived in Israel he would not have been allowed to captain an army. A little Israelite slave girl worked in Naaman's household and told her master that Elisha, the prophet, could effect a cure. At first this important man felt humiliated when told to bathe in the Jordan. However, he gave in and so completely recovered he felt Israel's God must be the true one. He took home some earth from the riverside so he could kneel on it and worship. He was quite a long way from knowing that God can be worshipped anywhere.

Mark 1:29-34

Jesus healed people according to their needs rather than their deserts. At the same time he made clear there is a great deal to be learned within suffering and sometimes this is the only way. Our Lord's disciples had to come to terms with the fact that all healing does not come easily. It may have to be struggled for in ways the sufferer would not have chosen. Some cures have to be prayed about for a long time and with great pain. Others never come at all. This was true for our Lord himself. Yet he was always able to adopt a positive attitude towards suffering and his love for us can help us cope with many a crisis which we could not manage in our own strength.

Prayer

I'm wondering, Lord, if life was ever meant to work out fairly. I'm thinking of people known to me who never seem to be really well. There are others who hardly know what it is like ever to feel off-colour. It does seem hard that some folk start off with so many disadvantages. It must be so difficult to keep cheerful when every movement is an effort, even if you can move at all. Do you expect the same amount of faith from us all, Lord? I think you rather look to each one of us to make the best of our own particular circumstances. It must be true that more is demanded of those whose path is easy. I've a feeling there is no way out of some of life's difficulties, Lord.....just a way through the mystery with you holding our hands because you had it all to learn too. If you could make a triumph even out of your cross, you must be the only one who can help us find victory when everything points towards defeat. I want to pray for some of my friends whose answer to prayer always seems to be "No". I can sympathise because I've been through the same frustration. So did you Lord and that is the comforting thought able to help me and those I love. AMEN.

OPEN YOUR EYES AND SEE

2 Kings 6:8-17

The ancient prophets spent a lot of time giving warnings. At one point, the king of Syria was marching against Israel and hoping to find the nation unprepared for war. However, Elisha warned Israel's king and the Syrians suspected somebody was betraying them. Suspicion fell on Elisha who fled with his young servant. This young man became very alarmed when he saw the army of the enemy coming very near. His master prayed the young man's eyes might be opened to the real situation. The enemy was near, but so was Israel's God and the mountains were filled with the hosts of the Lord.

Hebrews 11:32 - 12:2

Many of the New Testament letters were written to awaken faith and help people act with courage. The writers could always point to those who had triumphed in the name of God and the new Christians were often reminded they should keep themselves aware of his wonder-working power. Yet they must not merely look back; they must also look around to the opportunities presented by their own situation. The God of their fathers was alive and active in their circumstances. Jesus himself never lost sight of God, however bad his day.

Prayer

Sometimes I seem to be surrounded by so much that is evil, Lord. I find myself being overwhelmed and then I have to look quickly to your strength. Deep down I still believe good will be triumphant in our world, but it seems to be taking an awful long time. Will you help me? Keep me aware of all the good things that are happening. Remind me many people do still care about honesty, integrity and fair play. Hundreds of families still love each other and even extend their love to those whom they contact every day. When I start to feel helpless I want you to invade my thoughts, Lord. Remind me of everything I can do to make sure even the most unpromising situation can result in good, if you are allowed to deal with it. Sometimes I want that to be through me. I know I'm too impatient, Lord. I take a long time to do something worthwhile and yet all too easily I let my life take a wrong turning. Guide my thinking so I may not be swept up into things I do not want to do. Take me along in your way and keep my eyes wide open so I do not stray into byways of my own choosing. AMEN.

TAKE IT TO THE LORD

2 Kings 19:14-19

Hezekiah was one of few Jewish kings who received good marks. At least he made an attempt to give Judah firm leadership in getting rid of heathen shrines and pagan beliefs. He had a bad moment when his enemies asked from where he gained his confidence. We know the answer because we read that, when he received bad news in a letter, Hezekiah spread the scroll before the Lord. Evil had threatened this king's people so often and they had to be very sure God was upholding them all day and every day.

Matthew 26:39-42

None of us has ever prayed like Jesus did in the Garden of Gethsemane. He had made his plans and done his best to carry them out but now it seemed there was no escape from the way of suffering. So our Lord went to the only place he could for comfort. He laid his sorrow before his Father and we can almost hear the cry of anguish as he pleaded for help. Help came, but release did not. The cup of suffering had to be drained and, in a great effort of will, Jesus accepted this was the price he had to pay for love of mankind.

Prayer

It seems a bit ordinary to pray for common sense, Lord. Yet sometimes that is all I need. I know quite well where I should go and what I should do. In a way, that kind of prayer is easy. Yet there are many other days when I struggle in prayer and almost give up altogether. Help me to see your grace and love are not limited by the depth of my problem. Neither are they regulated by whatever mood I'm in when I come to you for help. When I think of Jesus praying before he died, I realise all my trials are so small compared with his. Yet the same deep strength is available for me as you gave to him. Remind me there is no point in pretending with you. You know me far better than I know myself. You are aware of the points where I may crack and you are there in my deepest need even before I pour it out to you. My Saviour really prayed; he didn't just talk to you. Please open me to everything you want to see about me. Then help me rest and trust before I take up the next challenge. AMEN.

FATHER FORGIVE

2 Kings 23:1-4

King Josiah was only eight years old when he succeeded to his throne in Jerusalem. He had a rather bad start as both his father and his grandfather had multiplied the heathen shrines and encouraged the worship of foreign gods. As soon as the young king was old enough to take decisions, he threw out all the idols. Even then the writer of the story tells us God's wrath was not appeased. It seems God still demanded justice. We realise what a lot had to happen before king and people learned to know God not only as judge but also as a caring Father who offered them forgiving love.

Matthew 21:12-17

We have a precious picture of Jesus visiting the Temple when he was only twelve. At that point he was asking a lot of questions and seeking to know his Father's will for the future. Later on, we see Jesus in the Temple again, and this time he knows many of the answers to life's problems. Jesus swept the Temple clean from all the cheating that went on at the money tables. At that point he could have stored up bitter hatred for those who insulted God in this way. Yet, even in his last few moments, he could ask for forgiveness, knowing God loves even the worst sinner.

Prayer

I am amazed how you could ask forgiveness, Lord, for those who cared nothing for God's will and even tried to silence you when you wanted to help them. I'm glad you felt the need to cleanse the Temple, but you did not leave it empty. You put all you had into trying to tell your listeners about the love of God, and that you had come to reveal it. When I come to you to pray, I so easily slip into asking for things. I realise if I invite you into my life, the first thing you will want to do is cast out much that is evil. Only then can you be the way to the Father. I want to think of other people here, Lord. I've harboured so many grudges and looked out for opportunities to get my own back. I know I must give forgiving love as well as receive it. You told us in one sentence that loving God and loving others must all go together. If I take a stand, Lord, I know I shall often be the odd one out. Remind me how brave you were in the face of testing and remind me, however strong the temptation, you have wrestled with it and won. AMEN.

WALLS WITHIN WALLS

Nehemiah 2:1-8

Nehemiah was personal assistant to the Persian king when news filtered through from Jerusalem that exiles returning home needed help. Nehemiah was given permission to go and proved very astute in using everybody's skill in re-building the city walls. One feels they must have used stones and rubble from previous buildings even as they drew strength from their precious religious inheritance. Yet, in a way, it is sad they felt the need to enclose the city. They had not yet learned that although God loved them in a rather special way, they must not cut themselves off from everybody else.

Revelation 21:15-23

John saw a splendid vision of a day when the teaching of Jesus would finally triumph over all evil. In the New Jerusalem the measurements have an extra dimension. This is no city which can be measured by mere height and depth. There is breadth too and this is the best way John can think of to describe something completely new. Inside the city we see all nations, kindreds and tongues. There are no restrictions and no limits. Even pain and sorrow have gone for ever. However much we try to place limits on the love of God, we see here that eventually it will prove to be the strongest power in all the world and beyond.

Prayer

I can understand why Nehemiah encouraged your people to rebuild the walls of Jerusalem, Lord. They had returned from exile and their beautiful city was a pile of rubble. They felt building strong walls might mean everybody could be safe inside and then they would be able to start all over again in their national life. We act rather like that when we encourage people to join the Church. We can then teach them and, in some measure, remove them from temptation. It comes as something of a shock when we realise you challenged us to go outside our precious buildings and look for lost people. Sometimes we may have to spend a lot of time with them, serving those who are lonely, hungry or living in some kind of sin. Thankfully, we can still get together for worship and others may come with us, but we must not stay there all the time. You spent days in your local synagogue, Lord, and we know you were happy to visit the Temple in Jerusalem. However, you turned the building upside down when you felt the people were not in line with your Father's will. When you gave your life for us you were outside the city walls and your nearest companions were two thieves. AMEN.

MY GOD.....WHY?

Job 42:1-6

The book of Job is more than an attempt to answer the problem of suffering. The problem remains a mystery; it is Job's attitude that changes. This happens as he comes to terms with his pain and his sorrow. Job lived at a time when it was believed that only good men prospered. If a person suffered, he must have sinned very badly. Job was not beaten by this argument put forward by his, so called, clever friends. He knew they were wrong, even when he could not answer them. He came through to a deeper faith and only then knew peace of mind.

Romans 8:31-39

Paul had plenty of opportunity to observe people who suffered. We also think he was ill himself quite often. He certainly took his share of the suffering that came because of persecution. Yet, when he wrote to the Christians in Rome, he was still able to believe everything was working out for good. He saw a close relationship with God for everyone who loves him, whatever their circumstances. He also knew Jesus is right beside us because he has been through far more sorrow than we could ever know.

Prayer

I know every experience of life should teach me about you, Lord, yet so often the experience overwhelms me. A pain proves too much, a bereavement too hard to bear. Help me to understand that even suffering and sorrow can be used in your hands, so the end result is good. I can think of wonderful happenings in my life which came about because other people were willing to suffer hardship. Keep me mindful of faithful servants of yours who were able to triumph even in the most unpromising circumstances. Parents, friends and teachers gave up a lot for me and I was not always grateful. Days when I suffered in some way could have meant I prayed more, but I did not use them. Talking of giving up, Lord, you surrendered so very much for me. Your pains were overwhelming but you prayed for us all as you went through them. Your loneliness must have been unbearable, yet you had no self pity and saw all that happened to you as within the will of your Father. I don't want to take everything you did for me for granted. I can't really say "Thank you", but I want you to give me a grateful heart. On sad days, help me to find you knowing full well that when I'm hurting most of all this does not mean you have gone away. AMEN.

LOVE CONQUERS ALL

Psalm 32

The psalmist is happy in the realisation he has confessed his sins and been forgiven. Then he tells how miserable he was before he made his confession. He expresses confidence in God and recommends the practice of prayer. God, in his turn, gives wise counsel and encouragement to trust. It is evident God expects his followers to learn from everything they experience. They are not animals to be forced with a bridle to go in a certain direction. They are human beings who can reject God's love which surrounds them and guides them.

Luke 15:25-32

The story of the prodigal son and the ever-loving father helps me understand what Jesus meant by real forgiveness. The boy was accepted back into the family long before he asked. However, he did need to turn his back on his sinful life and go home before the relationship could be fully restored. The only person badly left out was the elder son who would not forgive his brother. The faithful service he had given was commended but was not enough in itself. Love at the heart of the family was what the father cherished most. He showed this to both sons in ways their differing characters needed.

Prayer

Sometimes I wish you would force me to be good, Lord. Life would be so much easier if, when temptations come, you would encourage me to look the other way. However, I know that would make me like a puppet on a string. Deep down I am glad I can choose. It was when the prodigal son came to himself he wanted to turn round and go back home. Nobody forced him to abandon his sinful city life - least of all the father. His real self knew he should be at home with the family doing his share of the work as eagerly as he had asked for his share of the money. I know what pulls me back when I have wandered off, Lord. Your deep love for me draws me like a magnet and my horrible disobedient self shows up so badly. I want to be the person you intended and this strengthens my love for you because I realise this can never happen if I am far away from you. Take me home again when I stray, Lord. Give me work to do for you knowing full well this must be done with love if it is to be worth anything at all. AMEN.

PROGRESS IN FAITH

Psalm 40

The psalmist reveals he only found it possible to progress towards a mature faith one step at a time. He had to wait for God, during which period he obviously suffered. Gradually God helped him from his slough of despondency and set his feet on firm ground. Then he was able to sing a new song of praise to his God. He gave up belief that some kind of burnt offering would put him right and moved to the certainty that he must dedicate his life to doing God's will. However, his cry for help had to go on all the time.

Philippians 1:1-11

Philippi was one of the few churches for which Paul could thank God every time he thought about the people. They had learned a lot about the life and teaching of Jesus and Paul was able to help them follow their Lord even more closely. It is from Philippi we learn the word *koinonia* which means coming together in a rich sharing fellowship. The apostle's prayer for these dedicated people was that they would progress even further in the Christian faith. He wanted them to develop in knowledge, perception and trust so they could encourage other Christians who had not moved as far.

Prayer

I'm glad living the Christian life means I should grow more mature, Lord. It's time I stopped praying the prayers of my childhood. I know I had to start there but I must go on to face difficult problems which means re-consecrating myself to you over and over again. There is always a step ahead I could take but so often I try to avoid it, preferring to remain comfortable. This never works for long because you find new ways of challenging me. The psalmist learnt how to throw away his convenient offering and give you what you always wanted most - a heart full of love and a life offered for service. Jesus taught that lesson over and over again and the early preachers had to train the new believers into this new way of thinking. Most people could buy a lamb or a dove for sacrifice but you want living souls and dedicated workers. I sometimes ask myself what my aims are for the day. I was able to follow you reasonably well yesterday but I must do better today. If this is hard, I only have to think for a few minutes about all you are constantly doing for me. A whole life dedicated to your service would not begin to repay you. AMEN.

WITH HIM IN TEMPTATION

Psalm 51

This penitential psalm, attributed to David, was often used in Temple worship. David was inclined to blame his heredity for his sins although he acknowledged his need for inward truth. He thought of the cleansing given to a leper made from herbs dipped in blood, but realised this type of cleansing was not enough. He also had some glimpse of God as a spiritual being and knew within temptation there lies a choice of good and evil. God will always influence us but never forces us to do good.

Matthew 4:1-11

The first three gospels make the point that Jesus was tempted straight after his baptism. He had to choose his method through which to work and turned his back on bribery, sensationalism and compromise. He chose the way of suffering and death and so triumphed over the devil. However, this was not the end of Satan's attempts to capture him. He was tested many times and even when he reached Gethsemane there was the temptation to escape. Testing times were with Jesus all through his earthly days, but his triumph opened up the way for ours.

Prayer

I'm ashamed to come to you today, Lord. I asked forgiveness from you before I slept last night. You gave me peace of mind yet I didn't get far along today's road before my thoughts started wandering in the wrong direction again. I know this is the point where I should look away and focus my thoughts on you. I am so very grateful life is a battle you have fought and won. The devil led you into the wilderness and made you several tempting offers. You turned away, but that was only the beginning. In no time he was back again trying harder and harder to lead you away from what you knew was God's will for you. This is exactly my own experience. I may win little battles with your help but evil powers do not like defeat. I want to make my prayer positive at this point. I want to remember when the devil tempted you to feed yourself, you made a new commitment to feed all who were hungry. When he tried to persuade you into self-glory, you made it plain only God is worthy of honour. However clever he was, you always had an answer. Let it be like that for me, Lord. You won't mind if I even quote your words and I know you will help me to mean them from my heart. AMEN.

THY WORD - MY LAMP

Psalm 119:105-112

In the psalms we are often shown belief in God as something for which to give thanks. We hear man praising God for his wonderful works and then bringing that praise right back to within his own soul. There is often joyful thanks when someone sees God at work in history and even more for what God has in store for his people. There is often an extra dimension when people give thanks even in times of trouble. It takes a very real faith to thank God for difficulties and realise even problems can be something to sing about!

Luke 23:44-46

Jesus quoted the psalms as he was dying. It is said every Jewish child was taught to say *"Into Thy hands I commend my spirit"* before he went to sleep. We have known nights when we were too tired or unhappy to say anything else. God's word was often a comfort to Jesus. He would certainly appreciate the thought that the Word of God can be a light to our feet and a lamp leading our way. His way was far darker than ours but his trust was far stronger. He is the one to guide us as he goes with us along any path we must travel.

Prayer

I am amazed at the wonders of creation, Lord. Your Word banished darkness; light came and this opened up the way for life to be formed. Then you looked at it all and pronounced it good. Yet we often pass by the beauty of your world. We become so busy with our own affairs and do not always give ourselves time to stand back in awe and worship. Yet I am even more amazed you bother with us. You spoke with power when you formed the world, but you also speak intimately to the people in it. Many noises clamour for attention but it is your still small voice that gives me comfort and peace. I want you to remind me to listen for you even if I can think of nothing to say in return. I am grateful for words of Scripture which often light up my path. I have often been strengthened when those who love me can pray with me. Our words blend in love for each other and for you. AMEN.

SEARCH FOR LIFE

Ecclesiastes 2:1-11

There seems to be quite a lot of negative teaching in this strange old book. We feel little urge to copy the elderly *"lecturer"* although we can learn from his mistakes. He set out to find happiness and looked first at wisdom. He found little reward in collecting knowledge and the pursuit of pleasure left him equally unsatisfied. Eventually he turned against life and became bitter. One feels if he could have forgotten his own desires and thought more about other people, much of what he looked for might have been granted to him as by-products

John 10:7-18

Jesus knew for a long time that he must eventually lose his life. He may have been facing up to this when he spoke of a grain of wheat falling into the ground. Because it died, new life could emerge. Later on Jesus spoke of going to his Father and travelling on ahead where his disciples could not go for the time being. Yet, because he gave so willingly and did not seek to preserve his own safety, we can say Jesus knew life to the full. His example teaches that if we look for life we don't find it. If we live it, or even surrender it..... we do.

Prayer

I want you to put my life in order, Lord. I have wasted a lot of time trying this and that and, in so doing, neglected many things you made it plain I should think about. I have been here and there and forgotten you advised slowing down sometimes, just like you had to do. I have sometimes neglected my health by packing too much in my day. I have starved my mind from good food by filling it with thoughts that do me no good at all. As for my spiritual being, the evil one never leaves that alone. I need reminding Paul said God needs our bodies for a temple. Mine has often been more like a collection of rubbish. I want you to open my eyes and show me where I am needed most. I want you to help me listen for voices crying in need. Most of all I want you to take possession of my thoughts so I can pray as you wish and give my response to what you are asking from me. Sometimes I forget my time on earth is a sacred trust. I am not here to do as I please and I need to come to you so often and ask you to take away what is unworthy. AMEN.

SEND ME

Isaiah 6:1-8

Isaiah was granted a vision of the Lord and straight away felt the need for purification in his personal life. God cleansed him and then made plain this experience was to become public. God needed someone to denounce the sins of the nation and Isaiah offered to take on this unenviable task. It would have been pleasant to stay in the Temple and enjoy the wonderful closeness with God over and over again. However, God needed Isaiah to leave the quiet and go into the busy city life where his message had to be stern but also hold the promise of a future deliverer.

Acts 10:9-16

Jesus had made plain he offered his love to all men, but Peter found it hard to accept Gentiles as part of the church. God gave Peter a very strange vision and he began to understand it was not for him to decide who was worthy of salvation. It was Peter's task to take the message of Jesus into the market place. Peter went to talk to Cornelius about it and this reminds us special visions usually mean we have to extend our witness.

Prayer

You have been very close to me today, Lord. My times of quiet gave me peace of mind and I felt I could forget the troubles of the world for a little while. Nobody interrupted my thoughts and the 'phone did not ring once. I could do with a few more days like that. Maybe then I could remain steadier than I do and not feel so used up at the end of the day. Yet I know what you are saying to me at this point. Quiet is lovely, but I am often needed to go where there is noise and restlessness. Peace is so strengthening but I must not stay within its comfort for too long. I'm glad you went apart by yourself sometimes, Lord, and you told your disciples to do the same. But you took them back again, ready to give their new found strength to people who needed it. I suppose it's all a question of balance, Lord. If I stay with the battles of life too long I know exactly what the result will be. On the other hand, I remember it was for the world you gave your life. I am only one person and although my privacy is precious, I know too well other people want me. You got it right, Lord. Let the serenity of today help me face what I know must happen next. AMEN.

HOPE FOR THE FUTURE

Isaiah 40:1-8

This Isaiah's message came at a point when the Jews badly needed a ray of hope. They were in exile. Much of their home country was desolate and their beloved Temple was in ruins. Even their Babylonian conquerors were under threat from the Persians. Many felt God had deserted them and that the heathen gods had triumphed. Liberation came from the most unexpected place. It was the Persian leader himself who allowed the Jews to go back home. God was going to help his people back to their own land and Jerusalem would once more become an honoured city.

John 14:1-7

Jesus spoke words of comfort to his disciples just at a point when he could so easily have given up hope. His enemies were very near and his followers sensed danger. Their questions revealed they were very afraid. Jesus did not take away the immediate problems. He knew what they must all face and there was no easy way out. He did, however, help them look ahead to a time when all would be well. They would live with him and this promise helped them to believe in a loving Father who was as much in charge of the future as he was of the present.

Prayer

Thank you, Lord, for giving your friendly words of comfort when you yourself needed somebody to stand by and help. I believe your sorrow was as real as mine is. I feel you were tempted to give up and those angels hovering near would have been so useful had you chosen to call them in. You had the pains of the whole world on your shoulders - yet you could still hope. All this means you can take me through my bad moments and make sure I am not overwhelmed by them. I need you so often to sustain me when I almost despair. I want you to feed my thoughts so I can go on believing even when I am not certain what the outcome of my trust in you will be. I know from past experience you will sometimes grant me what I ask, but there will be days when, in your wisdom, you give me what I need and what will prove best for me in the end. I am so grateful for the best knowledge of all. Whatever the future holds, you will be there. You share every day if I do not shut you out. Restrain me, Lord, when I am worried and take too many steps at a time.....or try to. One was quite enough for you. AMEN.

DIVINE INSPIRATION

Isaiah 61:1-4

When our Lord preached in the synagogue, he quoted from this passage. At this point of testing, he certainly needed to be divinely inspired. The words were written at a time of national despondency when the people were still recovering from the effects of being exiled. Economic troubles added more suffering when the Jews were tired and being badly harassed by their enemies. They found it hard to go on believing that God was teaching them a great deal and the future was still hopeful. Isaiah said the right thing when he promised the Messiah would come as an answer to their prayers.

Luke 4:16-21

The return to Nazareth came at a crucial point in our Lord's earthly ministry. At his temptations he had turned down the opportunity to become famous by doing something spectacular. Here, as he claims to fulfil Isaiah's prophecy, he makes plain he wishes to be a servant who will suffer for those he tries to help. Everybody's eyes were still on Jesus, expecting him to do something out of the ordinary. In time their interest turned to enmity as the words he spoke were not those the people wanted to hear.

Prayer

I've come to the conclusion some people take advantage of the fact they know I will forgive them when they hurt me. Now I must ask for a fresh start, Lord, before I make any more unkind statements. I try to accept when folk say they are sorry but I know I harbour little grudges so I'm all ready to flare up again. That isn't kind to you, Lord, and all sin is against you not me. I act so in line with my feelings. If I'm cross I let everybody know about it and a whole lot more suffering is spread around. You coped so well with feelings and went about giving your love and asking so little in return. I want to keep looking at you. Only then can I say "No" to temptation and "Yes" to a kind deed that will help someone who needs me. There is something wrong with my judgement. So often the word or action that is unkind seems much more attractive than the good. I'm pretty hopeless when I turn away from you. In this quiet moment, I want you to take me over and sort me out. Only then can I live to anything like your standards. AMEN.

FAITH IN THE FUTURE

Jeremiah 32:1-8

Jeremiah is often thought of as a sad prophet. However, there was one day when he showed supreme courage. His country had been invaded by an enemy and a strong army was marching on Jerusalem. Jeremiah was in prison at the time but managed to negotiate the purchase of a field from his cousin who went to visit him. The prophet paid over the money and accepted the title deeds of the land. He hid these safely away in an earthenware jar which could be hidden in the ground and left there till happier times. In this way he put a stake in the future, trusting God to bring his hopes to fulfilment.

Revelation 21:1-4

We are helped to understand a little of the imagery of the book of Revelation if we remember for whom it was written and something of what was happening at the time. Christians were being persecuted and it seemed evil had the whole world in its grip. Beasts is not too strong a word to describe the despots striving for power. Within this seemingly hopeless situation, John bravely pointed out to the churches where they were going wrong. He also helped them to look forward to the time when all nations would gather in splendour at the throne of God.

Prayer

One of my hardest lessons, Lord, is learning to live one day at a time. I start worrying about tomorrow long before I should and so I carry more than I need through today. I want to be so sure of your love that I can leave the days to come in your hands and so make the most of the present moment. Yet there are times when it is good to look forward. Your people of old often kept themselves going by thinking of their promised Messiah. It always seems strange to us that many of them missed him when he came. No doubt this was partly because they were looking for the wrong kind of deliverer. The real Jesus rode on a donkey, not on a war horse, and the deliverance he brought was from inward sin rather than outward circumstances. I know the future need not trouble me. You are as truly there as you are in the present. I am thinking just now about those for whom the days to come hold little promise. Nations have been destitute for so long it is difficult to think of anything better. Many individuals hardly dare think of the future because their life has collapsed around them. Deal with those who feel hopeless very tenderly please Lord, and help me to do the same. AMEN.

TRY AGAIN

Jeremiah 36:1-4,20-23

Jeremiah was born into a priestly family. A reading of his prophecies also reveals him as a lover of country life. Sometimes, however, this shy man had to go into the city and give the king some stern words from God. Jeremiah struggled against this unpleasant task and dictated God's words to a scribe. The king was so furious about what was written on the scroll that he ripped it to pieces with a penknife and threw God's message into the fire. Jeremiah dictated it all over again and added yet more strong words from the Lord.

Mark 8:34-38

Jesus must often have been tempted to run out of patience with those he tried to teach. He often made the right way of living quite plain, yet his listeners still acted quite contrary to what he advised. Jesus loved them enough to persist, realising even grown men and women have to learn their lessons over and over again. Jesus never gave up with what he knew to be right, but made plain to his followers that following him would mean suffering. When this came, many ran away but almost all of them went back.

Prayer

I feel very safe with you, Lord. There is so much happening around me which pains me even to look. I don't want to get involved. I love the shelter of my Christian home and worshipping you with my Christian friends gives me so much joy. I feel you are interrupting that train of thought, Lord. You are telling me I must not hide myself away from problems. You loved sharing peaceful times with your disciples, but sometimes you walked straight into trouble knowing full well what would happen. I hate being unpopular, but you don't seem to have bothered about that for one moment. Even more, I am not at all good at putting up with pain. How did you bear the whip lashes without complaining? Those nails must have been just agony for you, let alone the indignity of being spat on. The worst I could go through wouldn't compare with your sorrow. I am trying very hard to ask you to give me something difficult to do for you today, Lord. I'll do my best to answer that call. Then I'll come home to you for comfort and maybe I'll even ask for another opportunity tomorrow. AMEN.

BREATH OF LIFE

Ezekiel 37:1-4

Ezekiel was an original thinker. This is evident when we try to understand his writing and feel we have wandered into a world of strange fantasies. We can sense something of the majesty of God as we see him on his chariot throne. We realise the need to take in what God says as we see the prophet eating the scroll. We understand more about punishment as the prophet shaves his head. We get a tremendous lot further in our knowledge of God in the story of the dry bones. We are thankful God can breathe new life into nations and individuals who might otherwise be lost forever.

Acts 2:1-12

It is good to remember Pentecost came to an ordinary room and to ordinary people. They were, however, very expectant people ready to receive. This was the end of their time of waiting and doubt. From now on they could preach and teach in the name of the Lord, confident of his abiding presence. The breath of new life gave them power to face a world which was hostile in the extreme. The Upper Room may have been small, and the world outside very big, but God's people were infused with new strength and could go out in faith.

Prayer

I feel you have had to breathe new life into your people many times, Lord. The nation into which you were born often required fresh invigorating power and your church also sometimes grows tired. Our prayers are often much too full of our own requirements when we should be asking for new life, new energy and deeper consecration to do your work in the world. The first Pentecost must have been quite frightening in some ways. Tongues of fire and mighty winds are not a regular part of our every day experiences. We can understand the symbolism. Fire is cleansing and wind makes us think of a mighty force. Your church needs both, Lord, if we would make a real and lasting input of new life for your world. So often the blockage is in us. All too often we are feeble in our witness and give up so easily when there are problems. Help us to come together in prayer and worship like your disciples did in the Upper Room. Give us expectancy and open our hearts and lives so we are ready and dedicated to tell the world of the wonderful thing you did by giving us Jesus. AMEN.

BUT IF NOT

Daniel 3:16-27

Nebuchadnezzar's fiery furnace was always very hot, but it was seven times hotter than usual when Shadrach, Meshach and Abednigo were thrown into the flames. These men had so strong a faith they refused to answer the king when he threatened them. They preferred to use their last words to affirm their faith in God. Yet they went on to say that even if God did not set them free, they would still believe in him. They knew God had the power to provide a way of escape but at that moment they could not be quite sure whether or not they would die for their faith as many others had done before and since.

Matthew 27:45-50

Jesus knew the physical pain which seems far worse at those moments when God feels far away. The amazing thing is Jesus chose to go through his suffering. He did not call for angels, accept the drugged wine nor come down from the cross. He did not curse those who were responsible for his anguish. All these things he could have done, but he accepted the complete sacrifice in order to show us the love he has for mankind has no limits. It goes the whole way and he gave himself to the full.

Prayer

I've had a bad patch today, Lord. I half listened to a conversation when the speaker was running you down. I've heard it all before, but this time I butted in. I meant well, but much of what I said didn't really help at all. I realised later I had started to feel sorry for myself and I quite lost sight of how it all started. Tomorrow I must try and put it right. I realise to my shame the best way to witness for you is to watch my lifestyle. This is often more important than what I say. Now I've another problem. I'm feeling some kind of pride because I'm suffering on your behalf. I know Christians are called to go through this at times, but there is something wrong if I get satisfaction out of it. So much of your pain was physical, Lord. You must have longed to fight back even though the situation was pretty hopeless. You didn't even blame your persecutors and at times you even remained quiet. That strange old story about the men in the fiery furnace reminds me that whatever I go through in life, you are in it with me. If I needed any further proof, your life on earth gives it to me over and over again, not to mention your final sacrifice. Next time I make a mistake.....tell me yet again that anything I do on your behalf must be done in your way. AMEN.

OPEN TO GOD

Daniel 6:7-10

Daniel lived at a time when the kings were prepared to sink to any depths to gain power. One tried a fiery furnace and another laid on a magnificent banquet where the golden vessels were stolen from the house of the Lord. That night, strange writings appeared on the wall and the king was murdered soon afterwards. King Darius followed him and at least he listened to Daniel. However, Daniel made more enemies because he foretold the future and they persuaded the king to throw Daniel into the lion's den. No harm came to him and he could still be seen praying before an open window.

Acts 20:7-12

The early church had not been established long before it became hard for people to gather for worship. The authorities locked up the leaders and hunted out the followers of the Way of Jesus many times. Yet the Christians still met together, even when persecution cost the lives of many of their friends. The little group at Troas is just one picture we have of the light of the gospel shining out for all to see. Lots of little lamps could be seen through open windows and meant everyone could see the family and their friends were meeting with their Lord.

Prayer

Sometimes I like to keep quiet about being one of your followers, Lord. Somebody might laugh at me or say horrible things about you. I'll be a Christian, but I'd rather keep behind the scenes. It's a good thing many of your friends have been braver than that through the years. I can read of some who went out of their way to make it plain they would believe in you whatever the cost. I can think of others who kept very close to you and even went into situations where they knew there would be problems. I tend to shut myself away. They opened their windows, stood on street corners and even went into the enemy's camp to make it quite plain whose they were and whom they served. I must pray for courage to stand up and be counted. I must give up doing only what is convenient and easy when tests of my loyalty to you are part of my day. It's so easy to compromise. It is so convenient to say "I'll do so much but no more." Yet deep down I want you to have all of me. In my better moments I want to return in some measure the love you gave me in so much fulness. AMEN

REDEEMING LOVE

Hosea 3:1-5

Hosea went through the bitter experience of being deserted by his wife. Yet he found grace to forgive her. In this personal trouble Hosea learned a lot about God's relationship with Israel. The prophet's message of redeeming love did a little more towards preparing the way for the One who would demonstrate it to the full. He was, however, aware that God's love contains judgement. Everything God is willing to give is available for the sinner, but this does not mean he will turn a blind eye to the sin.

Matthew 18:21-22

Jesus taught his disciples they must deal mercifully with those who wronged them. Only then could they themselves ask to be forgiven. Peter needed this message as much as any of them. He so easily acted without thinking and hurt other people as well as his Lord. Yet Peter was also very sensitive and took time to absorb the fact he must go on forgiving many times. Our Lord was trying to teach Peter and the others there must be no limits to forgiveness, even as there was no limit to the extent to which Jesus would go to show how much he loved them.

Prayer

I love a lot of people, Lord, but I like to choose them. Then I think about the way you give yourself to others and I find you place no limits at all. You could go into a town and straight away deal with everybody's needs. Your disciples hurt you so much, just as I do, yet you welcomed them back and trusted them all over again. Judas died after betraying you. No doubt at that point he felt you could never have faith in him again. I have a feeling you would have still loved him had he given you the chance. Peter cried when you looked at him after he had denied you. He knew you still cared and then felt so bad about letting you down. It wasn't all that long before he was preaching the Pentecost sermon. This drastic change was repeated in men's lives over and over again. This happens every time someone realises the depth of your love for them. There are many arguments against becoming one of your followers but the big thing which overweighs everything else is that you love us.....all the time. AMEN.

NEED FOR A SAVIOUR

Joel 2:10-14

Writings like this in the Old Testament help us see the need for the New. Joel saw judgement coming and likened it to a plague of locusts sweeping the land clean from vegetation. The Day of the Lord would be terrible and only God's faithful would escape. The heathen would stand trial but Israel would receive some reward for her faithfulness. Joel saw little hope for any nation except his own. Yet even he saw God as having some mercy. He also saw the need for sacrifice. Striking though this man's pronouncements are, they are a very long way from the message Jesus was coming to proclaim.

Luke 1:26-33

God tried many ways of communicating with his people through the years. Some of his words spoken through the prophets were frightening and terrible. These men had to think within the limitations of their own time and they found it impossible to realise God covers all time and beyond it. Eventually, God chose a new and much more tender way to speak to mankind. He came to live among them in the person of Jesus. God was still Judge, but he also revealed a heart full of love even for those who hurt him most.

Prayer

I am fascinated by the way you gradually made yourself known, Lord. I am very thankful I don't have to go back to the time when you seemed almost unapproachable. I can start much further on because Jesus came to show you to all who would look. Because of his teaching and living I can see you never intended your loving to be restricted to one nation. He made it quite plain everybody is your concern. Even though I love the tender way Jesus dealt with men, I know I must not ignore the very stern commands you gave to your early followers. It is still wrong to kill, steal and commit all those sins you warned against. I am thankful Jesus taught it is not enough to refrain from evil, we must also do good. If I can in some measure love you and my neighbour as Jesus did, my life will be transformed. Yet I must remember you are Judge as well as Father and I must look at Jesus every time I feel I am slipping into something downright wrong or very doubtful. Jesus very firmly said "Get behind me Satan". Then he was free to open his arms to all who needed him as much as I do. AMEN.

COSTLY WITNESS

Amos 5:10-15

Amos was a shepherd in the very desolate region of Dekoa and city life must have seemed far removed from his own meagre existence. Yet he felt compelled to make a public appearance at Bethel and there denounce so much that was displeasing to God. Religion in the city was at a really low ebb and was becoming a mere cloak to hide many doubtful practices. Amos not only faced the limelight himself; he was also the instrument God used to reveal a good deal the city authorities would have preferred to keep hidden. His only reward was to be thrown out.

Luke 18:31-34

The days Jesus spent with his disciples were on the whole happy ones as long as they remained in Galilee. Crowds followed; many people were healed and lifted up into new strength. Our Lord knew this could not last. He knew he must go to Jerusalem and this could only mean trouble for himself and those who followed him. Jesus went straight into the thick of threats against him, even to the Temple itself. There he showed up so much that was wrong in civil and religious life as well as within the human heart. Although he took his life in his hands, Jerusalem presented a challenge Jesus would not ignore.

Prayer

Sometimes I feel I belong with Old Testament people, Lord. I can't understand why wicked people did not perish. Your prophets did warn them they couldn't flout the ways of God forever. I need to be careful how I think here. I must be truly concerned that good will triumph over evil, not just work off some hurt to myself. I sometimes find it easier to point out other people's faults rather than face up to my own. This is where I have to move on into the teaching of Jesus. In spite of all he went through, he never tried to get his own back. He pointed out where people were going wrong but he always stressed some positive good that could come if men trusted him enough. When he spoke to the dying thief he did not dwell on the man's sins. He recognised a tiny shred of faith and told the man he would go to Heaven. This is so different from the way I often feel. I'm almost pleased when I see someone who has done wrong getting what I feel are their just deserts. Then I try to turn this back on myself and realise how badly I fall short of your standards. Supposing I got my deserts! AMEN.

FEW WORDS

Obadiah 1-4

In this, the smallest book in the Old Testament, we meet a man about whom we know very little. His nation was at enmity with her neighbour and, when Jerusalem fell, the Edomites occupied Israel's territory. Eventually, it was Edom's turn to suffer and her land was overcome by Arabs. The little book of Obadiah is not so much gloating as accepting the truth that God cannot be ignored for ever. Sooner or later retribution will come. God holds the future whether men choose to recognise the fact or not. So this little word says a lot.

Luke 23:6-9

When Jesus stood before Pilate, one word could have floored all the accusations against him. He said nothing. He knew if he faced his accusers in the way they wished, they would immediately think up something else. His manner made the hypocrisy of his trial very plain. Jesus made no claims which might have eased his way out of the trap. He did, however, say some very searching words from the cross. Most telling of all is that even at the moment of extreme suffering he asked forgiveness for those who inflicted it. Not retribution, just self-giving love.

Prayer

I often feel tempted to say "I told you so" when somebody reaps the results of wrong-doing. Your prophets of old must often have felt like that, Lord. You used them all to predict what would happen to nations which turned a blind eye to your ways. Sometimes they lived to see this happen; sometimes retribution came many years later. I've seen the same thing happen to individuals. I have to confess I've had moments when I've had to admit "I was warned". You yourself gave many warnings, Lord. This did not mean you permitted your followers to call down fire onto a district that was committing many sins, but refusing to listen to what your men were saying to try and stop them. You were so wise in the way you spoke to those who were going sadly wrong. That rich young man didn't want to be put right so he went away. Yet you still loved him. Right to the very end you did not ask for punishment for those who hurt you so much. You either kept quiet or made plain forgiveness was available. I know I must sometimes give warnings, Lord, but let me think it all out first and make sure my words and actions do not add to the problems. AMEN.

CHALLENGE TO MISSION

Jonah 4:6-11

It is a pity the whale has tended to take over the Jonah story, especially as the Bible does not mention it. The creature involved was a big fish and any schoolboy knows a whale is a mammal. The whole point here is that God wanted Jonah to do an unpleasant job in Nineveh and he did his best to get out of it. Later on Jonah grew more sensitive and even felt sorry for a plant because it was too hot. God was then able to make him understand he must also give help to a city that was getting far away from God's purposes.

Acts 15:36-41

Paul was sometimes reluctant to give backsliders a chance to do better. He was annoyed with John Mark who had an attack of homesickness during a missionary journey. Mark was forgiven later on but at the time it was Barnabas who saved the situation. Mark needed to have a second chance because God wanted to use him in the future. His home was going to be a shelter for the Early Church and his writings were going to be read by millions of people in the years to come. God wanted John Mark as a missionary in spite of his one-time weakness and with careful help he was able to answer the call.

Prayer

I like quick results, Lord, especially when I try to influence somebody else. I like quick answers to my prayers and I always want you to say "Yes." I find it hard to take set-backs and long-suffering with other people is certainly not one of my virtues. I find it hard to accept that good things will only get done in your time. Yet I expect you to be endlessly patient with me. Over and over again you have made your will plain and I have deliberately looked the other way or closed my eyes completely. Help me to develop some of the persistence practised by your prophets. They had to go to the people many times with your message and so many things happened which meant every move seemed to be in the wrong direction. This applied even more to your ministry, Lord. You were always much more than one step ahead of your disciples. When you called them to follow they pretended they didn't hear just like I do. They even ran away. I pray I may never do that. Your work is urgent, Lord, but time is in your hands and I must wait for your leading and guidance. AMEN.

PATIENT LOVE

Micah 6:1-8

Micah was a village man and disliked the towns where he saw much corruption and where strong people gained power by oppressing the weak. He saw punishment coming but could look beyond that to a day when God would have a people more worthy of his care. Micah reminded everyone how patient God had been with their sins and then poured scorn on mere outward shows of religion that did not result in justice, mercy and walking humbly with God. His prayer was that the Lord himself would help his followers become more obedient to his will.

Matthew 5:21-24

Jesus made it plain men could always go to God and be sure of being received. He also expected them to prepare themselves for worship. A man was not allowed to go anywhere near the altar if he had neglected to put right the relationship between himself and his brother. He knew we all fall short of that very often. Jesus talked about only the pure in heart being able to see God and we all fail there. It soon becomes evident that even if we try our best to remove any hindrance between ourselves and God, only he can make us anything like fit enough to go into his presence.

Prayer

I am wondering whether I dare come to you, Lord. I have often said my prayers without thinking very deeply about what I was doing. Sometimes my worship has been a mere formality. I want you to help me realise it is deep down within me where honour is due to you. Yet, on the other hand, I know I must not only worship you in private. I see there is a whole world full of people who need my patient love just as much as I need yours. Please help me into a new pattern of living so I can be more like you. You were so close to God all the time yet you gave yourself completely to all who came to you. I often remember you said we shall only see God if our hearts are pure. I feel this means I shall never get there. My heart is far from clean and my motives, even for good works, are often far from pure. I am so grateful you also said there is cleansing available for all who ask to be forgiven for their sins. That promise cost you an awful lot and I would not presume upon it. You will need to keep working on me, Lord. I need forgiveness and a chance to try again so very often. AMEN.

NEW LAWS FOR OLD

Nahum 1:1-8

Nahum's message came at a time when the Assyrian conquerors of his nation had themselves been devastated by the Babylonians. Israel had often prayed for the fall of her enemies so now she could rejoice. Nahum had little pity for the fallen enemy but just now and then we come across a more tender thought in his prophecy. *"The Lord is good." "The Lord is slow to anger."* God never acts in a hurry and every nation must bow to his justice even as they give thanks that he sometimes has to deal in what seems a drastic way. This may be the only method to let people know he is displeased.

Matthew 5:38-48

The Jewish people did not find it any easier than we do to accept they must sometimes expect bad treatment from others and even invite more. The teaching of Jesus was a long way removed from the old law that one could take an eye for an eye and a tooth for a tooth. That really meant one shouldn't take more. Jesus tried to drive home the point that at times we must expect to be treated harshly and even insulted. This was exactly what he himself suffered so why should we expect an easier passage through life?

Prayer

I am so glad you pray for us, Lord. There are so many things I cannot pray about because I have not reached a sufficient state of grace. I do not find it easy to love those who hurt me and I'm a very long way from turning the other cheek. My relationship with others is nothing like you prayed for in the garden and I sometimes feel far away from you. Maybe this is because I am trying to put other people right rather than myself. It is so easy to decide what one's friends should be doing in a given circumstance. I often lack the courage to withdraw a hasty word and say a kind one instead. So often I stop my service to you at the point where it begins to hurt. You are a kind Father but I know I must also think of you as Judge. It is for you to put other people right especially when I feel I am so good at it! I only have to take one look at the life of Jesus to realise how many black spots there are in my own. Forgive me if I sometimes try to work out who are your enemies and what should happen to them. Bring me back to the words of Jesus when he told us to love even those who hurt us. We all hurt you and so we need you to go on praying. AMEN.

WAIT FOR IT

Habbakuk 2:1-3

A commentary on this little book was found among the Dead Sea scrolls. This sheds some light about the time during which the book was written. The prophet questioned God's wisdom and could not understand why ruthless pagans were not punished for their sins. He felt too much injustice in the world seemed to pass unnoticed. God assured him he need not lose his vision for a better future even if its fulfilment seemed a long way off. The prophet was encouraged to write a psalm of praise as he waited.

John 11:5-15

Jesus loved Mary and Martha very much so it must have seemed hard when he kept them waiting for their miracle. He did not go to their home immediately. What happened when the miracle came was to have far-reaching effects - some of them very hard for Jesus. There would be a reaction from the authorities and giving new life to Lazarus was going to bring Jesus himself nearer to death. So he delayed things a little, seeming to emphasise the tremendous fact that he was giving a pledge he would eventually offer eternal life to us all. Only a few people realised Jesus had begun to show himself as Life itself.

Prayer

Forgive me, Lord, for not being willing to wait your time for answers to my prayers. I find myself doubting your wisdom and forget you can see the finished picture which is veiled from my eyes. I may be asking the wrong things. I read in the gospels you always chose the right time for whatever you did - even to be born. Sometimes I find myself wanting to change your plan for my life. Then I find I am rushing everything instead of waiting until you make your will known to me. I remember all your saints had to have patience and I try to see a delayed blessing is just what I need in order to develop strength of character. I want a clear vision, Lord, to remind me what a wonderful world this could be if we all made ourselves willing to think under your direction and act where and when you wish. All this takes time, Lord, and so often I feel this is what I can least spare. Give me grace to stay still and think this out. Then maybe I'll realise so much you want to do could begin in me ..... but only when you are ready. AMEN.

LIFE MEANS HOPE

Zephaniah 3:17-20

The last few verses of the book of Zephaniah are so different from all that has gone before we might wonder if they were added by somebody else. A message of unrelieved gloom gives way to the thought that people had survived the influence of two bad kings. The new young king, Josiah, was trying to do better. He was not yet strong enough to put into practice many of the reforms which were suggested by the newly-found book of the law, but there was at least a ray of hope that he was going to try. Unrelieved gloom is not the final answer for those who believe that God will prevail.

John 16:29-33

The disciples were very afraid when our Lord talked about leaving them. They could not think of anything much worse. He warned they would be scattered and not able to rely on each other for support. Yet even a seemingly hopeless situation like this had its brighter side. It was going to mean the apostles would spread out and so the gospel would be taken to new areas. Thus began the world's missionary movement which still goes on. Even the dreadful thought that Jesus would not be with them in the flesh gave way to the certainty he would be with them in spirit wherever they went.

Prayer

I would like to spread a little cheer, Lord. Your world is so often depressed and anxious. Before I can help I need a deeper insight into your ways. So often when all seemed lost you sent a deliverer. Only you can help us not to become too submerged in economic problems and political upheavals. Many of us should constantly give thanks we are spared much of the suffering which millions of people carry every day. We need guidance too when we grow depressed about your Church. We become obsessed by numbers. It is not true all churches are empty, which many who don't attend rather like to believe. Many churches have more worshippers than ever before. If we look world-wide we can see your Church is spreading all the time, although we know some areas need our prayers and concern. I'm glad we can use modern methods of technology to broadcast your gospel around. Help us to show by the way we live that all is never lost, however desperate the situation. If this is to remain true we may have to face up to more sacrifice. That's what it meant for you, Lord. I want to claim your power to help me. I know this means I must accept your leading as well as your example, so I can be the right kind of influence wherever you need me. AMEN.

TOWARDS RENEWAL

Haggai 2:1-9

Haggai's special task was to encourage the people as they built their new Temple. They had found this loved building in ruins when they returned from exile. The state of their Temple stood for the condition of all their national life. Unfortunately, the prophet had to point out they seemed to be more concerned to build their own houses first. He called on them to put God first and his words proved so forceful the Temple was started within three weeks. God had meant everything in their history so it was only right to honour him in this way.

Acts 8:4-11

The people of God have needed renewal many times. Philip was one person whom God used to spread the gospel to the Samaritans. He was instrumental in the conversion of Simon the magician and able to instruct a eunuch towards baptism. Many would have considered these people to be right outside the faith. God's family gradually learned that no-one is beyond the reach of his love. This lesson is still a priority for modern Christians. Each of us must try to consolidate what is good and also proclaim a new challenge and fresh ways of service.

Prayer

When I read my Bible, Lord, I am amazed you always seemed to find the right person for the job of the moment. Those old prophets not only knew when to speak but so many times they acted, and made sure everybody else did too. I am quite sure you have something lined up for me, though I have often pretended I haven't heard what you were saying. I'd be frightened if it were a big task, and even more doubtful if what you need from me is going to cost a lot and mean far more dedication than I'm giving you at the moment. I always persuade myself I'm not a leader. I'll try to follow if someone else takes the heavy end. That isn't how you thought, Lord. You set the pace for your disciples and you gave your utmost, even to those who found every excuse not to follow you. I realise this very day could be a turning point in my life. This could be the time when everything I live for could take on a new meaning. What stops this from happening, Lord? I stop it myself by holding back what I could offer and turning a blind eye to going where you need me most. That's wrong I know and I'm trying very hard to overcome all my weakness and remember everything is possible with God - even transforming my life. AMEN.

QUESTION THEN SURRENDER

Malachi 3:1-7

This messenger of God took no dogmatic stand about what God was saying to the nation. He chose to speak through a series of questions. The people were disillusioned and weary with waiting for promises to be fulfilled, so they had plenty of questions to ask. The priests had become lazy and bored and couldn't do a lot about supplying the answers. The people were only making second-rate offerings to God and had almost forgotten their calling. The whole of their national life suffered and they needed reminding to turn back to the Lord.

Matthew 22:15-22

People often went to Jesus with questions. Sometimes this was a genuine attempt to find the truth. More often it was nothing more than an attempted trick. At one point, under the guise of trying to get out of paying their taxes, a group tried to make Jesus side either with God or with Caesar. Jesus made plain both are entitled to their own type of loyalty. His answer contained a reprimand and even those who tried to trick him knew full well that only by believing in Jesus would they find the truth about life and how to live it.

Prayer

I am remembering you claimed to be the Truth, Lord. This means when I come to you with questions, I must not have my mind already made up. You have the answers to all my problems, but I know you may want me to work out the details of the answer for myself. As I pray for guidance, I want you to help me keep your standards at the centre of my thinking. You have given me the precious gift of a mind and I ask you to help me use it only to your glory. Please forgive me when I have mistaken loyalties and go all out to follow some ideal which I feel in my heart could be wrong. My mind becomes baffled when so many opinions are thrust at me and I find myself wanting to accept the easiest. When I am bewildered, Lord, please bring me back to your feet. Like Mary, I know that is the only place to learn. Like Mary again, I want to give you my love in humble worship. I want my offering to be sincere and I know you will not ask more from me than I am capable of giving. When I question, please teach me to wait for the answer and go on believing you will rescue me in your own way and in your own time. AMEN.

GOD'S LINE OF PEOPLE

Matthew 1:17-21

Both Matthew and Luke give us the family line of Jesus. Matthew shows him as the promised Messiah, descended from David. Luke emphasises Joseph's ancestors. It is unusual to find women in the list, even more so that at least four of them had very doubtful characters. We have met many of the characters in the earlier pages of this book. It is astounding that it was out of this line that Jesus came. In many ways Jesus was like those who came before. In one way he was quite different. Jesus was without sin.

Hebrews 11:39 - 12:3

The early verses in this chapter of Hebrews give us a picture gallery showing people of faith. God made it plain he was proud of them, in spite of all their weaknesses. He used them in spite of their frailty and he loved them all the way through. These people of old looked forward to the day when God would fulfil his promises, although none of them lived to see it. This was because God chose to include us in his list of people. This only becomes possible because Jesus shared fully in our life. Truly he was one of us.

Prayer

Thank you for sharing life with us, Lord. Thank you for being one of us. This is such a help on bad days when we need to draw deeply on your strength. During happy times we know enriching joy and peace with you. We want to try to praise you for every experience of life, even when our hearts are heavy and we feel we have no voice to sing to your glory. You used some very strange people in the past, Lord. At least this gives me hope you could use me. Many of them knew only too well what was your will for them, but they turned away and took others with them. Some were brave and strong and faithful and we are glad to remember your Kingdom could spread because you used them. Now it is our turn, and we need constant guidance as we ask for our influence to be good and lasting. I am amazed at some of those you used, Lord. I would not have chosen them.....but then I'm so glad you have chosen me. You have often brought good out of seemingly hopeless situations. The only ones you couldn't use were those who spurned your love. I don't want to spurn it, Lord. I need it all day and every day, whatever I do and wherever I go. AMEN.